MW01264599

POEMS
IN THE PANDEMIC

DAVID KIM

I dedicate this book to my family — my immediate family and to the Garden Church family.

To my wife Sharon — you have been the best life partner given by God, serving God faithfully side by side with for the past 29 years! Living and serving you has been a ton of fun!

To Danny and Joel, I am so proud to be called your dad and am so proud of how you have become such stand up men of God.

I would also like to dedicate this to my mom in heaven who passed down the identity of a worshipper to me.

To the Garden Church family, what a journey it has been over the past 26 years! Am so thankful for each brother and sister in the Garden — you are bearing much fruit and making a great impact for the Kingdom!

Dear friends,

I am so excited to share with you these poems that were written during the time of the COVID-19 pandemic! When I turned 50 in 2019, the Lord put in my heart the desire to write songs and poems. Prior to that time, I had written a few songs and poems and raps (old school 80's rap style). In 2020, when COVID-19 hit, the Lord started to download poems into my heart and mind. He would wake me in the middle of the night and give me ideas for poems and the poems themselves. In the midst of the chaos of the Coronavirus, writing poems became an outlet for me to express my heart to God. I wanted to encourage the members of The Garden Church (the church where I have served as pastor for 26 years) during this tumultuous time. I posted my poems on Facebook and found they were an encouragement to people both inside and outside of our church. So I kept on writing poems, writing almost 200 poems during a seven-month period. My favorite character in the Bible is David (for whom I was named by my Godly mother who is with the Lord) who used poetry to worship the Lord and to encourage others. My prayer is that these poems may help facilitate fresh worship unto the Lord and bring encouragement to your souls.

In His Amazing Love,
David Kim

CONTENTS

In the Time of Covid

This chapter of poems is focused on the impact that Covid has had on all of us and how the Lord has been working powerfully in the midst of this tumultuous time. It's in these trying times where our faith in God becomes refined and strengthened.

Prayer

Lord keep us safe
From this deadly virus
Please protect our families
May Your Spirit guide us

We pray for all health workers
Those on the front lines
Serving others selflessly
Your love through them does shine

We pray for a quick end
To this global scourge
As we do our parts
To flatten this big curve

As we're in our homes
Help us to reflect
On the blessings You have given
From despair protect

Lord we'll make it through
With Your love and grace
In this time of Covid
We will seek Your Face!

3.30.20

Covid Revelation (Part 1)

Covid struck the world
And brought us to our knees
Rich and poor alike
Vulnerable to this disease

We're not in control
Like we think we are
A small little virus
Can totally alter

The course of our lives
What does it all mean?
What can I learn?
What truth can we glean?

There's only One to trust
It's God and God alone
All else will fail us
He is on the Throne

He is our Hope
An Anchor for our souls
His Name is Jesus
He is in control!

9.19.20. Serra Retreat

Covid Revelation (Part 2)

What can we learn
From COVID-19?
While we all wait
For the hoped for vaccine?

Life is a Gift
Given from Above
What's most important
Is living in LOVE

God is the One
In Whom we can trust
All of our treasures
Surely will rust

All of our plans
Our finite and flawed
Only God rules and reigns
Our control's a facade

Each day is a gift
To be lived to the full
Thankful for the lessons
Learned in Covid school!

10.22.20

LOVE

Greater love has none than this
To lay down one's life
Seen so clearly in the cross
Jesus' sacrifice

It's seen in others all around
Health workers in the front
Serving others selflessly
Taking on the brunt

Of Covid care, they show up
Serving day by day
Helping others to get well
While self is in harm's way

The love of God so beautiful
Flowing from the Throne
Flowing from the Father
Flowing through His own

Lord let Your love shine bright in us
Let the whole world know
As we sow Your seeds of love
Cause Your love to grow!

3.28.20

Love One Another

Love one another
Just as I loved you
Do unto others
The things you'd like for you

Washing other's feet
Putting others first
Serving those in need
Blessing when you're cursed

In these times of trial
Love is what we need
Love is the food
On which our souls can feed

Endless supply
That comes from above
It is the love of Christ
It's called agape love

Faith hope and love
These three things remain
Love is the greatest
Let's build a new love chain!

3.29.20

Thank You!

Thank you Essential Workers
We'd all like to say
For your faithful service
For your protection we pray

Thank you Healthcare Workers
Serving on frontlines
The Lord bless and keep you
On you may God's Face shine

Everyday heroes
Meeting people needs
Serving in this crisis
Showing your good deeds

We pray for your families
That they'll be safe and sound
We pray for their well being
For His blessings to abound

The best of humanity
Shining in this hour
Thank you for your service
May God's strength be your power!

4.13.20

SIX FEET

Six feet is the length
From others stay away
Times of social distancing
The rules we must obey

To keep from getting sick
Or making others ill
For Covid has no cure yet
They haven't found the pill

Though we are apart
We still can all connect
Instagram and Facebook
Others like to text

How times have changed
Things have gotten better(?)
When was the last time
That you received a letter?

In these crazy times
We are not alone
We'll get thru this together
We cannot on our own!

3.30.20

Your WORD

Your Word is a lamp
To guide us through the night
When we are in darkness
Your Word is the light

Your Word is the Truth
That sets our hearts free
Your Word is Life
That draws us near to Thee

Your Word brings Hope
Oh how we need it now
Live a life of victory
Your Word shows us how

Your Word contains the promise
Surely You will keep
Making good from evil
Joy to those who weep

I trust in Your Word
Lord I will obey
Your Word in times of Covid
Will guide us all the way!

3.31.20

HOPE

Hope is what we need
In this Covid trial
To keep our souls from sinking
To keep us all the while

We stay six feet apart
We shelter in our homes
Hope will be our anchor
We are not alone

It's not wishful thinking
A shot in the dark
Hope is based in Truth
Always hits the mark

Hope comes from Your Promise
Your Word which You will keep
Our souls are at rest
Hope gives peaceful sleep!

God of Hope now fill us
Hear Your people pray
We'll all make it thru this
Lead us day by day!

4.1.20

Please Wear A Mask!

Dear fellow Americans
Please wear a mask!
You're saving people's lives
Is it too much to ask?

Your rights are killing others
Wearing masks will slow the spread
Don't you care
That people will be dead?

I do believe in rights
But I believe in love
The greater law
Given from Above

Please listen to the science
And to common sense
We're ALL fighting Covid
Masks are our defense

Thanks for listening
This advice is free
I'm an at-risk person
Hear my humble plea!

6.20.20

Cure

Panic spreads
Nothing seems sure
Now's the time
To Know the Cure

Daily growing
Fear takes hold
Coronavirus
Story unfolds

He is not far
In fact He's near
Call on His Name
He will appear

When He responds
All fear is gone
He turns the darkness
Into dawn

His Name is Jesus
He is the Cure
He reigns on high
We are secure!

3.12.20

The Cross

Look upon the Cross
The place where Jesus died
Understanding the meaning
Why He was crucified

Jesus died for you
Jesus died for me
Took upon Himself
Our sins so we'd be free

Love personified
He laid down His life
So that we could live
And end all our strife

The Cross has the Power
For those who believe
To save a person's soul
A gift you can receive

So look to the Cross
And find salvation there
The cross is evidence
Of the God who cares

4.8.20

Holy Saturday
(The Day Between Good Friday and Easter Sunday)

Between the Cross and Resurrection
Lies Holy Saturday
Living in the tension
Intermission in the play

Grieving for His death
Waiting for His life
To swallow up the grave
Anxiety is rife

Will the Promise come
True on morrow's shore?
Feeling hope and fear
For what is in store

Surely He will rise
On the third day it's been said
Saturday is long
My worry starts to spread

I will wait and I will trust
I put my Hope in You
Oh Holy Saturday
Soon you will be through!

4.11.20

The Victory of Easter!

The Victory of Easter
News we need to hear
Proclaimed on the Cross
The message loud and clear

In His Resurrection
Jesus won the fight
Overcoming death
Changing history's plight

In this time of Covid
People filled with fear
Jesus won the victory
So come on people cheer!

This Good News is for all
The victory is yours
Just call on His Name
He can change your course

Billions in the world
Celebrate the Son
Jesus is the Victory
The battle has been won!

4.19.20

Calling All Prodigals

Calling all Prodigals
Those who've been away
The Father loves you dearly
Is waiting by the way

He's prepared a party
For you a special place
There is no condemnation
Only love and grace

When He sees you coming
The Father starts to run
Breaking all tradition
You're His beloved son! (or daughter!)

In this time of Covid
It's time now to come home
It's better in the Father's house
Than in the darkness roam

Amazing grace how sweet the sound
That saved a wretch like me
The song of the prodigals
His love will set you free!

4.9.20

HEAVEN

This world is not my home
I'm just a passin thru
Heaven's my true home
Eternity with You

You've prepared a place
For those who put their trust
In Your Cross and Resurrection
Believing is a must

No more tears and no more pain
A place of joy, delight
Seeing Jesus face to face
Everything's All Right

Reunited with mom and dad
They took an early flight
Death defeated, darkness gone
Lord You'll be our Light

Knowing Heaven waits for me
Gives me hope today
Until then I will live my life
Trusting in Your Way!

4.16.20

Pressing Reset

This is the time to Press Reset
Time to refresh our screens
Type in a new direction
A time to change the scenes

Clear away all of the muck
The haze that clouds our souls
Letting Light shine on our hearts
Breaking old strongholds

Reset relationship with God
Connecting to the One
God of Resurrection
Just say the Word, it's done!

Reset relationship with those
You love but seldom share
Tell them that you love them!
Show them that you care!

Live each day like it's your last
Make the moments count
Press reset and live your life
Build your love account!

4.19.20

bored out of my gourd

I'm bored out of my gourd
Zoomed out to the max
Trying to get some rest
Can't seem to relax

Watched too much news
Am going stir crazy
Already took a nap
I feel very lazy

What should I do?
Sitting in this chair
What day is it?
A haze is in the air

Don't even know
Why I write this poem
I know that there are others
I know I'm not alone

This day will soon pass
I'll wake up from my slumber
Hope this stay at home
Will end when we hit summer!

4.22.20

ZOOM

Social distancing
Brought a boom
Biggest craze
It's called Zoom

Zoom zoom zoom
The new classroom
Hours on end
It does consume

Have a meeting
In your shorts
In this life
Without sports

Click on mute
Play a tune
Turn off video
Leave the room

Life has changed
As we knew it
Zoom has helped us
All get through it!

4.23.20

Refresh Me, Lord

When I'm feeling weary
When my spirit's low
I need Your refreshing
To give me my mojo

Holy Spirit wind
Blow into my sails
Revive my heart and spirit
Bring a mighty gale

Of Resurrection Power
That raised Christ from the dead
Resurrect me Lord
Help me get out of bed!

To face the day with faith
To fight the good fight
To break down racist strongholds
To overcome the night

I feel Your strength within me
Returning once again
I know that You are with me
Until the very end!

6.27.20

Worry

Worry, worry all is blurry
Everything seems so surreal
Hypotheticals abound
The feelings felt are real

Tightness in my chest
Fear weighs me down
How can I find relief?
In worry will I drown?

What if I get sick?
Will Covid ever end?
These questions are like daggers
Worry's a dead end

"Do not worry" Jesus says
Can these Words be true?
God's eye is on the sparrow
Know He cares for you

Help me Lord to put my trust
Help worry go away
I feel the weight lift off my chest
This is the better way!

4.23.20

Face to Face

Face to face with myself
The showdown is now on
Cracks in surface now appear
With distractions gone

Like an onion many layers
Covering my heart
Digging deeper to the core
Breaking me apart

Excuses, blame find no firm ground
It's me, Lord, here I stand
Cover me, Lord, with Your grace
I lay down my demands

Finding rest, finding peace
Comfort in my skin
In the Kingdom way
Surrender is a win!

Face to face with myself
Has led me Lord to You
When I'm at my end
Is when I find breakthrough!

4.30.20

Ready to Return?

Coronavirus put on hold
The world has all pressed pause
Getting ready to go back
To life as it once was?

What is the new normal?
Coming out the gate
With all that time on zoom
How now to relate?

Hopefully we can all now be
Kinder and more real
More in tune with others
With how the other feels

Social distance, keeping safe
Six feet is the rule
We all are now new graduates
COVID-19 Home School!

As we all emerge
Hopefully the better
We're all on the same team
We're all in this together!

5.2.20

Waiting on the Lord

Those who wait on You
Will renew their strength
With wings like eagles
Extended to full length

Soaring in Your Presence
Living in Your love
Seeing things from higher up
Seeing from above

In Your Awesome Presence
Is fullness of joy
Pleasures at Your Right Hand
Filling up my void

Clock stands still when I'm with you
Eternity is here
A little glimpse of heaven
Worry disappears

Those who wait on you
Will not be put to shame
Living in Your freedom
Kindling our heart's flame!

5.5.20

Breathe

Exhale the fear
Anxiety
Breathe out the toxins
My soul's debris

Release the things
We can't control
He is GOD
That's HIS role

Breathe in His peace
Breathe in His love
Holy Spirit
Like a Dove

Rest upon us
Help us know
You are with us
Wherever we go

You give us breath
The air we breathe
In these times
To You we cleave!

6.24.20

Amazing Grace (personal version)

Amazing grace how sweet the sound
That saved a wretch like me
You sought me and You found me
Your truth has set me free

It's all by grace, Your favor Lord
Has brought me to my knees
Gladly I surrender
My pride is now released

The old has past, the new has come
I am a new creation
Your blood has washed away my sin
My soul sings with elation

Through many dangers, toils, and snares
Your Goodness brought me through
As I face my current trials
I put my trust in You

When we've been there ten thousand years
In our heav'nly home
We'll sing and dance, we'll give all praise
To the Lamb upon the Throne!

3.27.20

LIVES or MONEY?

Lives or money?
Government's in session
Don't they know
Life's more than our possessions?

Sheltering in place
Is surely saving lives!
Let's wait a little longer
So more people can survive!!!

Liberties must give
This is the way of love
Giving up our rights
Is what love is made of

We need to be united
We have been so thus far
Let's keep our focus strong
Love is our clear North Star

May we all choose what's right
Before our Loving Lord
God give us the strength
To walk in one accord!!!

5.6.20

Open Doors

God opens doors
That no man can shut
This brings us hope
When we're in a rut

He closes doors
That no man can open
He is the One
That we put our hope in

We know that He's good
Just look at the Cross
He laid down His life
We're no longer lost

In this pandemic
No matter how
You've been affected
Remember this now

The Lord God is with you
He holds Your Hand
Will guide you until
You reach Promised Land!

5.9.20

New Things!

Bring forth in my life
New things in the spring
Pandemic winter
Has come with a sting

Breathe on me afresh
Sweet Spirit of God
Bring forth new things
So our souls may be awed

By Your glory and power
By Your creative Hand
Lift up Your Name
Throughout this land

Write a new chapter
Lord in my book
Keep my thoughts filled
With Your great outlook

I'm looking forward
To see what You'll birth
In this pandemic
May Your praise fill the earth!

5.13.20

We're All in This Together!

We're all in this together!
In this Corona fight
We'll get thru this together
We're gonna be all right!

Doesn't matter rich or poor
The color of our skin
Covid's our common enemy
Covid will not win!

May we stay united
The theme of this new poem
Let's stop the spread of this disease
We're still safer at home!

A blessing that has come
Unexpectedly
We're loving one another
The me has turned to we!

Lord give us the strength
Help us live as one
Help us be united
Until the battle's won!

5.14.20

A QUARTER MILLION LIVES!

A quarter million lives lost
Each one a mother or son
Worldwide tragedy
Feels like Covid has won

Weep with those who weep
Cry with those in pain
We're STILL in this catastrophe
We'll never be the same

Lord bring Your comfort
Lord bring Your peace
Lord bring Your healing
May this suffering cease

We are the world
We sang decades ago
This time it's ALL of us
This virus doesn't know

The color of our skin
Covid affects all
We'll get thru this together
Lord, on Your Name we call!

5.14.20

God is Good All the Time!

God is good
All the time
He turns the water
Into wine

He's making good
Out of bad
Transforms our tears
He makes us glad

Through Corona
We're seeking Him
Finding Light
When things grow dim

We trust His goodness
In these times
Through this trial
Our souls refined

We praise you Lord
Through good and bad
Our faith in You
Is ironclad!

5.16.20

Spring

Spring's my favorite season
Hope is in the air
Gentle breeze is blowing
Thru my uncut hair

Flowers start their blooming
Birds begin to sing
Winter days are over
Praises to the King!

Coronavirus winter
With your gloom and doom
Spring brings resurrection
Leaving the empty tomb!

Lord bring forth new blossoms
In our lives this Spring
We'll declare Your goodness
Fresh testimonies ring

Lord of all the seasons
Of Winter, Summer, Fall
Thank you for the Spring
My favorite of all!

5.20.20

Immanuel!

God, You are with us
That is Your Name
Immanuel
Your promises we claim

Never will You leave us
Never will forsake
You are always working
When we sleep You're awake

Because You are with us
We will not fear
No matter what comes our way
What circumstance appears

We can do all things
Thru You Who gives us strength
Even this Coronavirus
No matter what its length

Immanuel!
Your goodness we proclaim
Thank You for Your Presence!
We bless Your Holy Name!

5.21.20

JESUS IS LORD!

2020 election
Causing all to worry
Whoever takes office
The future seems blurry

Look up to Heaven
Turn your face toward
The One on the Throne
Jesus is Lord!

He Rules and Reigns
He is not elected
Thru all of the chaos
His Lordship unaffected

He's our Rock in the quicksand
Our Refuge right now
Confess Him as Lord
Let your knee take a bow

Jesus is Lord!
He's Risen indeed
For 2020
I choose Him to lead!

11.2.20

Your Ways are Higher (Isaiah 55:8,9)

As the Heavens are higher
Than the earth below
Your ways are higher
I can be still and know

That You are God
You're in Control
This is the Truth
No need for a poll

In the midst of Corona
We will not fear
When things are uncertain
When vision's unclear

Your ways are Higher
You know what is best
When I doubt
My faith's put to test

I trust in Your Love!
Shown on the Cross
No matter what circumstance
Of gain or of loss!

11.22.20

Give Thanks!

Tis the time
For Thanksgiving!
When we count our blessings
Our hearts our brimming

With praise in our hearts
To our God who is good
He's good all the time
With Him we've withstood

Difficult times
And Difficult days
Giving to God
The Sacrifice of praise!

He's always with us
Thru thick and thin
When we praise Him
His Kingdom breaks in!

Give thanks to the Lord!
Let all join the song
On the day of Thanksgiving
And all the year long!

11.25.20

Gethsemane

Place of Surrender
Gethsemane
Not my will Lord
But let Thy will be

Done in my life
I yield to Your Way
Trusting Your Heart
No matter what may

Come down the pike
I'll take up my Cross
Following You
Is never a loss!

I'd rather have Jesus
More than anything
At this Holy Place
My life to you I bring

Freedom reigns
At Gethsemane
Free from myself
It's not about me!

11.29.20

Covid Time

Monday Wednesday Friday
Days are flying by
This is Covid Time
Normal does not apply

It's March then it is June!
Now we're in December?
What just happened?
Can't seem to remember

Feels like we are living
The movie Groundhog Day
Every day's the same
A never ending play

All this time at home
Is making me batty
Moody at times
And sometimes crabby

Covid time
Dragging on and on
Just like that
A whole year is gone!

David Kim 12.2.20

Covid Time REDEEMED

Monday Wednesday Friday
Everyday with You!
Covid Time Redeemed!
The Kingdom's breaking thru!

Longer quiet times
Less time on the road
Two way conversations
Revelation download

People are more open
To Kingdom things
Chances to share the Gospel
This Covid time brings!

More time with family
Safer at home
More time with Jesus
Coming to His Throne

Thriving not just surviving!
In this Covid Time
One day in His Courts
better than a thousand online!

David Kim 12.2.20

The Vaccine is Here!

A long time of waiting
And now the day has come!
The Vaccine is here!
Covid's day is done!

So many suffering
So many in fear
Coming to an end
For the Vaccine is here!

Not AstraZeneca
Or the drug from Pfizer
This Vaccine
Can't be found at Kaiser!

This Vaccine is greater
It works for all life's ills
This Vaccine is Jesus!
The Sin Curing Pill!

He died on the Cross
He rose from the grave
THE Vaccine is here!
For all He's come to save!

David Kim 12.7.20

Man's Best Friend

Tough day at work
And then I come home
Chopin's there to greet me!
And throw me a bone

Of unconditional love
Licking my face
Dogs are the best!
Furry models of grace

Always so happy
To be by my side
Always on my team
His loyalty's bonafide

Chopin is a warrior
Always guarding our pack
Chasing coyotes
Anything for a snack!

Sadly it's the time
To say my farewell
Chopin, how I'll miss you!
In my heart you'll always dwell!

David Kim 12.8.20

Covid Advent

Covid Advent season
Has a deeper meaning
Most are in their homes
Some are quarantining

Waiting for this time
To come to an end
World's been put on hold
Hoping to transcend

The trouble and the suffering
Our world's only Hope
The coming of the Savior
With Him we can cope

With any circumstance
He told us this would be!
In the world there's trouble
Victory's in Me!

Come Lord Jesus!
Our Immanuel!
God is truly with us
In Him our souls are well!

David Kim 12.13.20

Fruit of the Spirit

This chapter of poems is focused on the nine Fruit of the Spirit found in Galatians 5:22,23. The Lord has been cultivating these fruits in our lives during the time of the pandemic.

FRUIT OF THE SPIRIT: LOVE

Love is the First
Love is the Last
Love Never Fails
For God's Love is Vast

Love is not hidden
It must be seen
Beautifully defined
In 1 Corinthians 13

Agape is Pure
Unconditional Love
Love and Sacrifice
Fit like a glove

Love includes feeling
But is so much more
Love is an Action
God's Love restores

Love your Neighbor
As yourself
To our broken world
Will bring much needed health!

7.28.20

FRUIT OF THE SPIRIT: JOY

JOY is a Fruit
That we all enjoy
JOY's more than Feeling
JOY is Sugoi! (Awesome in Japanese)

Joy comes from Jesus
That is the Source
His Joy is My Strength
Powerful Force!

In His Presence
There's Fullness of Joy
In His Name
Depression is destroyed!

In this world we'll have trouble
But be of Good Cheer
He's Overcome!
We've nothing to fear!

Lord give us more JOY!
We need it today!
Your Kingdom come!
Do not delay!

7.28.20

FRUIT OF THE SPIRIT: PEACE

Peace is Shalom
Comes from Above
Peace is Wellness
Living in Love

Peace has the Power
To overcome fear
Peace is Trusting
That He is near

Lord guard my heart
And mind with Your Peace
I lay down my worry
My fretting must cease

Peace in these times
Of division, unrest
Sin of racism
Must be confessed

Lord bring Your Peace
To our world today
through Your People
Your Peace display!

7.28.20

FRUIT OF THE SPIRIT: PATIENCE

Lord give me Patience
I need it now!
Help me to straighten
My furrowed brow

Waiting is hard!
It's not easy to wait
Anxiety high
My teeth start to grate

Help me to know
That You're in control
I can exhale
Be still my soul!

As I wait I am growing
In Faith and in Trust
Patience is forming
Learning to adjust

Lord give me Patience
With You I will wait
Lord You are faithful
You won't be late!

7.29.20

THE FRUIT OF THE SPIRIT: KINDNESS

It's Your Kindness that leads us
To Repentance, O Lord
When we deserve judgment
You show Your Love toward

Us in our weakness
Us in our sin
Us in confusion
Struggling within

You're Rich in Mercy
You're Rich in Grace
You're Rich in Kindness
Our souls You embrace

You're Kind to the Leper
You're Kind to the Thief
You're Kind to the One
Who's swallowed in grief

Help me be Kind
To others today
You've shown me Kindness
I'll follow Your Way!

7.30.20

FRUIT OF THE SPIRIT: GOODNESS

God You are Good
You're Good all the time!
It's part of Your Nature
For You are Divine

There is no evil
Dwelling in You
You always do Right
You always are True

This world calls good evil
Says evil's okay
No moral compass
Continually astray

There is Right
And there is wrong
There is Good
We won't go along

With public opinion
Defining what's Good
We learn of Your Goodness
As declared in Your Word!

7.30.20

FRUIT OF THE SPIRIT: FAITHFULNESS

God You are Faithful
Your Promises True
There is no shadow
Of turning with You

What You say You will do
In Your Word we can rest
Knowing You do
always what's best

Making us more like Christ
Turning all things for good
God became Flesh
Moved in our neighborhood!

Faithful to us
Your children You are
Even when we
Stray and are far

I wanna be Faithful
I wanna be True
I want my whole life
To bring glory to You!

7.31.20

FRUIT OF THE SPIRIT: MEEKNESS

Meekness is not Weakness!
It's given a bad rap
Meekness is Strength
Lying under wraps

Jesus was Meek
Stayed quiet when mocked
Controlled His anger
When I would have socked

The mouth of my enemy
Jesus stayed chill
Submitted Himself
To His Father's Will

Help me to take
Your Yoke as my own
Help me to live
In Your Rest Zone

Blessed are the Meek
They'll inherit the earth
Your Kingdom runs counter
To this world's sense of worth!

7.31.20

FRUIT OF THE SPIRIT: SELF CONTROL

The Fruit of Self Control
How I need you in my life!
To win the war within
To quiet my soul's strife

To say no to the flesh
When it wants its way
To follow Holy Spirit
To live under His Sway

To beat my body
And make it my slave
In the day of trial
To temptation will not cave

To choose to do what's good
When evil is at hand
In the day of battle
In You I'll make my stand

The Fruit of Self Control
Growing Day by Day
One day will be a Crop
Of righteousness, I pray!

7.31.20

JUSTICE

During the time of the pandemic, racial tension and injustice have been brought to the forefront of our country with the murders of Ahmaud Arbery and George Floyd. Prior to this time, I had been silent about the matter of systemic racism against Blacks and other minorities in our country. The Lord convicted me to speak out on behalf of the oppressed as justice is a matter held near and dear to the heart of our Heavenly Father. These Justice poems helped me to express my thoughts and heart and advocate on behalf of the oppressed and suffering.

Worse Than Coronavirus

God our Father
Something's wrong
Why does justice
Take so long?

Precious brother
Killed in cold blood
While he's running
In neighborhood

Worse than Corona
Is this scourge
Disease of racism
We must purge

We all must stand
And be outraged
To not stand silent
Or stay backstage

Help us Lord
To live as one
To fight for justice
'Til love has won

5.8.20

History is Happening

History is happening
Right before our eyes
Our country is awakening
Hear the people's cries

Calling out for justice
Blood calls from the ground
We stand with Black Americans
Our voices join the sound

Weep with those who weep
The Body feels your pain
For far too long
Our silence is our shame

Lord we cry for mercy
For healing in the land
Brothers, sisters we unite
In Christ we make our stand

Thy Kingdom come, Thy will be done
On earth here in this hour
Break the holds of darkness
Holy Spirit move in power!

6.6.20

I Can't Breathe

I Can't Breathe
One man's cry
Ignored by four cops
Who made him die

Deadly wrong
Is this scene
Way too often
Happening

I Can't Breathe
A people's cry
Being choked
We wonder why

Racism.

This is our country's
Original sin
From the beginning
It has been

Alive and well
To this day
It must end
Lord, we pray!

5.28.20

More Than Ever Before

More than ever before
This world needs Jesus
He is the only One
Who can truly free us

Coronavirus
Systemic injustice
Plaguing our world
We're living in crisis

Anger and fear
Rage and sorrow
Watching the news
What happens tomorrow?

Jesus, help us!
Calm the raging the sea
Speak the Word
We'll listen to Thee

It's only Your love
That'll never fail
We look to Your Cross
How You took the nails

5.30.20

Wake Up, America!

Wake up, America!
It's time to face the facts
Racism is alive and well
Especially if you're Black

Make up, America!
For all the silent years
Not standing for justice
Giving in to fear

Break up, America!
Hardened hearts and minds
Not knowing we can't see
Not knowing we are blind

Speak up, America!
For those who have no voice
Stand for the oppressed
Boldly make the choice

Cry out, America!
To the Lord of justice
Lord, may Your mercy
Be poured out upon us!

5.31.20

SALVATION

Being "woke"
can be a joke
Just a bunch of smoke
Unless it leads to

Action
Gaining traction
Letting the Spirit guide
my reaction

Gotta chill
Be still
Discern His will
Ask Spirit to fill

My heart
Where it starts
Convicted
Torn apart

Broken over my sin
Over racism must win
Color of our skin
Shouldn't dictate

Our value
Redeemed by the Cross
Found when we were lost
Jesus paid the cost

For OUR SALVATION.

6.1.20

COURAGE

To stand for what is right
No matter what the cost
Courage is a virtue
Sadly today seems lost

To live out your convictions
To go against the flow
To stand with all or stand with none
Knowing what you know

To break out of our comfort
Out of status quo
To live with higher calling
To live life with gusto

Lord give us courage
As we follow You
Who laid down Your life for us
For us You have come through

We'll follow in Your footsteps
Taking up our cross
All the things we thought were gain
We now count as loss!

5.21.20

It's Time for Prayer!

Brother and sisters
It's Time for Prayer!
To pray against
The ruler of the air

Against flesh and blood
Our battle is not
With spiritual weapons
This war is fought

Behind racism
The spirit of hate
The spirit of murder
The enemy lies in wait

We must repent
And give no place
For the enemy
In our own space

The Name of Jesus
Above every name
Only through Him
Victory we claim!

6.3.20

In Memoriam of George Floyd

Today we grieve
Today we cry
To our Brother George Floyd
We say goodbye

Our nation mourns
We say your name
Know your death
Won't be in vain

Your murder has brought
Awakening
To a people's
Suffering

Systemic injustice
That must be changed
Power structures
Rearranged

Watch from heaven
The change that came
From your death
We're not the same!

6.4.20

Change Me, Lord

Change me, Lord
Help me to be
Filled with love
And empathy

Change our country, Lord
Help US to be
Filled with love
And unity

Part of Change
We must repent
Of the sin of racism
We do assent

Only You
Can bring the Change
Break our hearts, Lord
Please exchange

Our hearts of stone
To hearts of flesh
Holy Spirit,
Fall afresh!

6.8.20

8:46

8:46
The time it took to kill
Have you watched the video?
And you wonder, still?

Why there is an outrage
Protests in the land
Crying out for change
Justice our demand

Our Brother George Floyd
The world will say your name
Along with all the others killed
They did not die in vain

Let's all now take a knee
Bowed to God in prayer
Praying to our Father
The pain He knows and shares

For change to truly happen
We must first change our hearts
We're all in this together
We all must play a part!

6.9.20

A Time to Listen

This is a time to Listen
This is a time to hear
To press into the Shepherd
May His voice be clear

This is a time to Listen
To the voice of those in pain
Black brothers and sisters
From you we can obtain

Your stories of injustice
Centuries of wrong
The story still being written
Been going far too long

It's time for a new chapter
This country's due for shift
For people who're downtrodden
It's time for real uplift

This is a time to listen
God's Word speaks the way
Say the Word, Lord, and it's done
You have the Final Say!

6.10.20

Sound of Revival

Black, White
Yellow, Brown
ALL the peoples
Hear the sound

Sounds of Revival
Coming near
Blowing thru
The atmosphere

Bringing repentance
Prepare the way
Bringing forth
A brand new day

At the cross
Is level ground
We all are lost
Need to be found

Send Revival
Start with me
Then let it spread
Through our country!

6.12.20

The Color of Unity

Neither Black nor White
The Color is Red
It's the Color of Unity
The Blood that Jesus shed

Crimson stained Cross
Brought peace to man
With us and our Creator
Gave us a place to stand

This Blood makes a bridge
Between all the races
Jesus' forgiveness
Gives us the basis

To love our neighbors
As ourselves in Him
He gives the strength
When our supply runs thin

Lord we plead Your Blood
It's the only answer
To remove this country's
Racism cancer!

6.13.20

A New Song

All can join the chorus
A new song in the land
2020 rendition
Of He's got the whole world in His Hands

You dwell in our songs
There's power when we praise
Yahweh Nissi, we call on You
Your Banner we will raise

When Paul and Silas praised You
The ground began to shake
When this nation starts to praise You
The chains will start to break!

King David knew of worship
A slingshot and a lyre
Taking out Goliath
Lifting Yahweh higher

Most High God we worship
We bless Your Holy Name
We build a fresh new altar
Send Your Holy Flame!

6.15.20

A Place to Stand

Here I stand, I can do no other
Martin Luther said
I find my anchor in God's Word
His Words are my bread

Where can I stand when hell breaks loose
When country's lost its way
Your Word's a plumb line for us all
Gives guidance for today

All other ground is sinking sand
World's philosophies
Conservative or liberal
These cannot set us free

There is a Rock higher than I
A Rock that will not fail
You took on all of our sin
The Cross God's justice scale

Thank you Lord for giving us
A place where we can stand
People of God let's all arise
Bring justice to this land!

6.20.20

God Bless America

God bless America
Land that I love
In this day of reckoning
We find what we're made of

Cleanse us from our history
From our racist roots
Liberty for all
History refutes

Look into the past
Look into today
From the evil of slavery
To getting pulled over by the way

Blessed is the country
Who puts her trust in Thee
Who owns up when confronted
The truth will set us free

We pray for Your protection
We pray for Your Shalom
God bless America
My home sweet home!

6.20.20

Empathy

Help me Lord to feel
To share another's woe
Teach me Empathy
To leave my status quo

Help me Lord to see
From others' point of view
To look beyond the surface
From others' lens see thru

To feel beyond myself
How things affect just me
Like the Good Samaritan
To live compassionately

To be Your hands and feet
To be Your beating heart
To listen and to learn
This is where we start

Black brothers and sisters
We see you in your pain
We are all One Family
Under God's great Reign!

6.24.20

Indifference

Keep me from Indifference
A heart that does not care
A life that's self-enclosed
A life that's unaware

Hardened heart affects me
My arteries are clogged
Racism cholesterol
I'm living in a fog

How can I declare
That God lives in me?
When I don't care for others
And live indifferently?

We must put an end
To this hypocrisy
Let's live like we say
Let's live what we believe

Lord we need a miracle
Only You can change our hearts
We rededicate ourselves
For You we're set apart!

6.24.20

With Kingdom Eyes

Help me see
with Kingdom eyes
To see your value
To realize

The Imago Dei
That lives in you
Worth His Blood
Highest value

I see you are
His Work of art
His Masterpiece
Made from His heart

I see the pain
That you've been thru
I see His grace
That's carried you

I see you
Do you see me?
In His love
We are free!

6.28.20

Imago Dei (The Image of God)

Created by the Creator
His Image is in you
In all of Your beauty
His Glory shining thru

You are Very Good
I hear the Lord God say
You are My Beloved
My love you will display

The Imago Dei
Made to be like Him
Agape love fills our hearts
Flowing o'er the brim!

Unity in Diversity
Loving all the same
A miracle that's possible
We pray in Jesus' Name

Dear Heavenly Father
In times like these we pray
Your children, every one of them
Lead us in Your Way!

7.2.20

Aaron and Hur

When Moses raised his hands
As he stood up on the hill
Joshua was winning
The fight below until

Moses' hands grew tired
Then the battle turned its course
Joshua was losing
Lost his Spirit force

Then Aaron and Hur arrived
To support their friend
To lift up Moses' hands
Fresh strength they did send

May we be Aaron and Hur
To our Black family
Lifting up their hands
In Solidarity

Jehovah Nissi fight for us
The battle belongs to You
Overcoming racism
The Victory's in view!

7.5.20

This poem was inspired by Pastor Phil Allen's prophetic prayer over
our church to be an Aaron and Hur to the Black community in this
kairos time.

My Brother's Keeper

I am my Brother's Keeper
My Brother I will keep
I rejoice when you're rejoicing
Am weeping when you weep

To my Black brothers and sisters
I hear you in your pain
I stand with you as family
Your gain is My gain

To love as Jesus loved
The call upon us all
To care from the heart
Love for the long haul

What would this world look like?
If we all heed the call
To be our Brother's Keeper
Justice would not stall

Though Cain said no, we say yes!
Lord we will obey
We'll be our Brother's Keeper
The calling starts Today!

7.12.20

Washing Feet

Jesus showed the Way
Washing His disciples' feet
Giving an example
Making things concrete

Lowliest of tasks
Done by God Most High
We're called to do the same
Our selfishness deny

What does it mean to wash
Another's feet today?
To help those in need
To go out of our way

To care for the poor
To lift the oppressed
To look beyond ourselves
And our self interest

Lord we heed the call
To wash another's feet
In serving one another
Our love is made complete!

7.16.20

Who Is My Neighbor?

Who is my neighbor?
The tricky lawyer asked
Jesus made it clear
Took the man to task

Love like this Samaritan
Who cared from his heart
Compassion from the Father
This is where we start

He loved his natural enemy
The one who hated him
Overcoming racism
The color of his skin

May we heed the call
To be Good Samaritans
May THIS be what defines
All Americans!

With our Black Neighbors
We shall stand side by side
Till justice shall prevail
In love we're unified!

7.16.20

Poems on the Psalms

This chapter is focused on the poems inspired from the book of Psalms. King David is my favorite character in the Bible. In his psalms, he expresses his heart to God in rawness and honesty. The Psalm 23 poems are inspired by each verse of this classic psalm.

I Shall Not Want (Based on Psalm 23)

The Lord is my Shepherd
I shall not want
Is there an exception
Written in small font?

To meet all my needs
To heal all my pain
Too good to be true?
Too much to claim?

Your Presence is Real!
Your Promise is True!
Pearl of great price
Of Highest Value

To know You in truth
To take in Your love
Greater than anything
This world can know of

Lord I believe!
My doubts I confront
The Lord is my Shepherd
I shall not want!

7.9.20

Green Pastures (Based on Psalm 23)

Good Shepherd lead me
To Green Pastures today
Satisfy soul hunger
With Words that allay

My desire to seek
The things of this world
That leave me empty
My soul unfurled

Your Word is like honey
Your Words are so sweet
Your Words are real food
I delight to eat

Your Words are my comfort
Your Words are my help
Five star review
I'll post on Yelp!

You lead me to
Green Pastures today
My soul satisfied
All trouble at bay!

7.9.20

By Still Waters (Based on Psalm 23)

Lead me to rest
By the Still Waters
A place of refreshing
For Your sons and daughters

Hearing the sounds
Calming my soul
Gently reviving
Making me whole

May inside reflect
The outside I see
Still waters outside
Still waters in me

In times of turmoil
Where things are so tense
Lead me to You
Your peace be a fence

Around my heart
And around my mind
By the Still Waters
Rest I will find!

7.4.20

Paths of Righteousness (Based on Psalm 23)

Lead us into paths
Of righteousness today
Good Shepherd, please help us
We all have lost our way

Lead us into justice
Bring change in our land
Holy Spirit fill us
Help us take a stand

Lead us into prayer
The greatest power on earth
We ask in Your Name
Our country needs rebirth

Lead us to Revival
Dry bones come alive
Form the Lord's new army
In crisis we will thrive

Lead us Lord to You
Our praises will ascend
The Alpha and Omega
Beginning and the End!

6.13.20

Restore My Soul (Based on Psalm 23)

When my heart
Is heavy laden
The world around me
Being caved in

Where can I go
To restore my soul
To fill this wounded
Gaping hole

Negativity
All around
Everyday
Distress abounds

There is a place
Of quiet rest
Near God's heart
The place most blessed

Restore my soul
ABBA Father
Hear my cry
My soul will prosper!

7.6.20

Thru the Valley (Based on Psalm 23)

Even though I walk thru
The Valley of death
I fear no evil
For You give me breath

You breathe Your peace in me
I exhale my fear
My soul is at rest
For I know You are near

Because You are with me
I can face everything
COVID-19
Or whatever life brings

Racial injustice
And all kinds of hate
You've been thru it all
You can relate

Thru the Valley is Growth
Your Presence a Must
I will get thru
In You I will trust!

7.11.20

Thy Rod and Thy Staff (Based on Psalm 23)

Thy Rod and Thy Staff
They comfort me
Bringing protection
From enemies

Giving me guidance
When I lose my way
I am a sheep
Often I stray

Pulling me out
Of troubling times
Disciplining me
That I might align

To the way of love
To become more like You
Helping me see
From Your point of view

With Thy Rod and Staff
You prod and You pull
These tools you employ
To bring Life to the full!

7.11.20

You Prepare A Table (Based on Psalm 23)

You Prepare a Table
In the midst of my enemies
Love them as my neighbors?
The ones who have hurt me?

When I was Your enemy
You died on the Cross
To overcome the breach
It came at such a cost

On the Cross you took
All my sin and shame
You bore my penalty
Blessed be Your Name!

We need to set a Table
All are welcome here
Mercy on the menu
Your Love casts out all fear

Good Shepherd You are seated
At the Head of the Table
Where everyone is loved
Regardless of all labels

7.12.20

You Anoint My Head with Oil (Based on Psalm 23)

You Anoint My Head with Oil
My cup overflows
Righteousness, peace and joy
Your Spirit bestows

Greater things than these
We'll do in Jesus' Name
Miracles abound
When Your Kingdom is proclaimed

Your Anointing is Real
Abiding in me
Guiding in all Truth
Making blind eyes see

Holy Spirit
You are welcome here
Come flood this world
Make hate disappear

You Anoint My Head with Oil
I am overflowing
Into this hurting world
Your Spirit Wind is blowing!

7.13.20

Surely Goodness and Mercy (Based on Psalm 23)

Surely Goodness and Mercy
Will follow all my days
Lighting up my path
Setting my heart ablaze

With gratitude and thanksgiving
Lord how good You are!
Faithful to your people
Alabanzas exclamar!

God is so good
He's so very good to me
This song I will sing
Into eternity

Mercy over judgement
The Cross the Final Word
This Good News must be known!
Around the world be heard!

In my rear view mirror
I see Goodness and Mercy
Good Shepherd in my vision
I am worry free!

7.13.20

I Will Dwell in Your House (Based on Psalm 23)

I will Dwell in Your House
The place I want to be
In this world I am homeless
My true Home is in Thee

Like Abraham I live in tents
Looking for True Home
Worshipping in Spirit and Truth
Where You build Your Throne

We're Your House, the place You dwell
Your people are the place
Your Glory Cloud comes down
When we seek Your Face

Living Stones, we are Your Temple
Built upon the Rock
Offering spiritual sacrifices
May our walk match our talk!

Dwelling in Your House
One day is better than
A thousand elsewhere anywhere
Your Kingdom is At Hand!

7.15.20

Forever and Ever! (Based on Psalm 23)

Forever and Ever, that's a long time!
Will Heaven ever be boring?
Playing our harps upon the clouds
Won't that leave us snoring?

Yes that would! But not the case!
Heaven's Full of JOY!
Unconstrained by time
His Presence we'll enjoy!

Every Tribe, Nation and Tongue
Joining round the Throne
Giving praise unto the Lamb
Who made us all His own

He'll wipe away every tear
Death has lost its sting
Love abounding everywhere
Better than anything

Than we've experienced here on earth
Heaven will surely be
An eternal celebration!
We wait expectantly!

7.15.20

Psalm Minus 23

The Lord is NOT my shepherd
I'm constantly in fear
Living in the desert
My way is seldom clear

I go to get water
Yet I'm thirsty still
Following my desires
Following MY will

When I'm in the valley
I feel all alone
Wondering who will guide me
Who will bring me home

I make my own table
With enemies and friends
I eat and drink to heart's content
Not thinking of the end

In my life I'm living
I know what is best
Hoping one day that I can find
A place my soul can rest

3.25.20

Blessed (Based on Psalm 1)

Blessed is the one
Who does not walk in fear
Trusting in Your Word
When things aren't so clear

Planted by the stream
Roots down in good soil
Holding steady, standing firm
Amidst all turmoil

Delighting in Your Word
Dwelling day and night
Seeing the invisible
Walking by faith not sight

Standing like a tree
Leaves of evergreen
Bear fruit that all enjoy
From Canaan's land we glean

Lord in every season
Your garden's in Your care
Paradise lost has come again
Hope is in the air!

3.18.20

Be Still and Know (Based on Psalm 46)

Even though the earth give way
And in the raging sea
I will not fear for you are near
Your praise will ever be

On my lips, I will declare
That You are Lord of all
Rescue me, when I'm afraid
Lord hear me when I call

I will be still and know that You
Are God, and You Alone
Reign on high, Your Kingdom come
You sit upon the Throne

I come before Your Throne of Grace
Find mercy in my need
Peace that guards my heart and mind
By Your power I am freed

Be exalted Lord in all the earth
Let all the peoples know
There is a River whose streams make glad
From Whom all blessings flow!

3.18.20

Dwelling in The Shelter (Based on Psalm 91)

Dwelling in the shelter
Of the shadow of Your wings
Lord You are my Refuge
To You my soul clings

Protected from the arrows
Of fear that fly by night
Lord You are my Fortress
My faith in You my sight

Lord command Your angels
To guard us in this time
Keep us from this pestilence
Lord protect our minds

From thoughts of panic, fear, despair
Running through our head
Help us Lord to trust Your Word
The things that You have said

You will rescue us O Lord
You will hear our cry
Dwelling in Your shelter
Of the One Most High!

4.4.20

I Lift My Eyes Up (Based on Psalm 121)

I lift my eyes up to the hills
I put my trust in Thee
You do not slumber, nor do You sleep
You're my soul's PPE

You will not let my foot give way
Protect me from all harm
I find my resting place in You
In Your loving arms

You are the Maker of heaven and earth
You are God Alone
In this time of world chaos
I'll let Your Name be Known

The things of earth will fade away
What then does remain?
Loving others as You have loved
Serving in Your Name

Keep us safe, watch over us
Our coming and our going
While we shelter in our homes
Keep our souls growing!

4.5.20

NAMES OF GOD

The Scripture tells us that "the name of the Lord is a fortified tower; the righteous run to it and are safe." (Proverbs 18:10). These poems on the Names of God focus on the many Names of God found in the Scriptures and how we can personally experience the different facets of the character of God.

Names of God: Elohim - Powerful God (Genesis 1)

Let There Be Light!
And there was Light!
ELOHIM's Power
ELOHIM's Might

GOD the Creator
You Rule over all
Brought us Redemption
When we took a Fall

You Created the Heavens
You Created the Earth
You Created Humans
Gave them their Worth

When I look at the Heavens
And all You have made
My Soul starts to Worship
Your Majesty Displayed

ELOHIM You are Worthy
Of all my praise
I glorify You
All of my days!

8.2.20

Names of God: Jehovah - Covenantal God (Exodus 3)

You spoke to Moses
Revealed Your Personal Name
I AM THAT I AM
Forever the Same

I AM JEHOVAH
Forever will be
I bring Your Deliverance
I part the seas

With Moses My Friend
I spoke Face to Face
Showed him My Glory
Showed him My Grace

To all who would know Me
Hear My Invitation
I AM your God
You are My Creation

I keep My Promise
with those who believe
I AM JEVOHAH
My blessings receive!

8.8.20

Names of God: Jehovah Jireh - God Our Provider (Genesis 22)

Jehovah Jireh
You provide all my needs
Generous provision
Does not include my greeds

On Mt. Moriah
Provided a ram
Foreshadowing
The dying of the Lamb

You Who Gave Your Son
Freely gives us all things
You're a Good Good Father
Every good gift You bring

Ask and it is given
Seek and you will find
You love to Bless Your children
You are so Rich and Kind!

O Jehovah Jireh!
Thank You for being You!
Faithful to Your People
Always coming through!

8.8.20

Names of God: Jehovah Rapha – God is our Healer (Exodus 15)

You are My Healer
You heal me through and through
Jehovah Rapha
My wholeness come from You

You heal every sickness
Every disease
By Your Stripes I am healed
I fall down on my knees

In worship, Lord, I praise You
You heal every pain
Turn mourning into dancing
You give me joy that remains

You're the same today forever
But doubt has been a thief
Lord I believe!
Help my unbelief!

I put my trust in you
Jehovah Rapha, now!
I lay hold of Your healing
On bended knee I bow!

8.9.20

Names of God: Jehovah Shalom - God is Our Peace (Judges 6)

Jehovah Shalom
God You are my Peace
In these crazy times
May there be a Cease-

Fire of the hate
Division and divide
True Peace comes from You
When in You we abide

Jehovah Shalom!
We call on You, we pray
In our racial turmoil
May Justice have its day

Made Peace with us thru Jesus
His death on the Cross
The bridge to the still waters
For us you suffered loss

Thank You for Your Peace
Without You we are lost
Without You we can't live
Your Peace Life's Secret Sauce!

8.11.20

Names of God: Jehovah Nissi - The Lord Our Banner (Exodus 17)

Jehovah Nissi Our Banner!
The Battle belongs to you
When I'm feeling down
You overcome my blues

The Victory of Jesus
Accomplished on the Cross
Vanquished satan once for all
Defeated his weak sauce

When Moses raised His hands
In prayer to God Most High
Joshua won the battle
Your mighty power was nigh

Lord we pray for Victory
In our world today
Overcome the darkness
Bring back those who stray

Hallelujah You have won!
The Victory is Yours!
Jehovah Nissi we proclaim
Victory is sure!

8.11.20

Names of God: Jehovah Rohi - The Lord Our Shepherd (Psalm 23)

Jehovah Rohi
Good Shepherd to me
Laid down Your life
Proved Your love, eternally

I'm in Your care
I shall not want
You protect me from harm
When the enemy taunts

I lie down and rest
My cares cast on You
My sleep is sweet
Dream the night thru

When one sheep goes wandering
You leave the 99
You will not rest
Till the lost one you find

I was the one
Now I join you on Your search
To find the lost sheep
And bring them back to church!

8.11.20

Names of God: Jehovah M'kaddesh - The God Who Sanctifies (Leviticus 20)

Jehovah M'kaddesh
The God who changes me
I once was blind
But now I can see

Lord You are Holy
There is none like You
In You there is no darkness
In You all is True

Make me more like Jesus
Change me from within
Expand my compassion
Help me to hate sin

Transform my thinking
By the renewing of my mind
Shedding worldly values
Leave materialism behind

I'll be fully changed
When I see you Face to Face
Until then I press on
Living on Your Grace!

8.11.20

Names of God: Jehovah Tsidkenu - The Lord Our Righteousness (Jeremiah 23)

Jehovah Tsidkenu
Lord Our Righteousness
Imputed on the Cross
Your Throne of Grace access

Though my sins were scarlet
Now I'm white as snow
I'm clean and forgiven
Praises overflow!

When I was Your enemy
You broke thru my defense
Took my sin upon you
Melted my pretense

Took me out of Egypt
Into the Promised Land
Not just a story
I've experienced You first hand!

By grace I have been saved
Nothing I have done
Jehovah Tsidkenu
My heart You have won!

8.11.20

Names of God: Jehovah Shammah - God Who is There (Ezekiel 48)

You are Jehovah Shammah
You're the God Who's There
You are Omnipresent
Here, there, everywhere!

Where can I go from Your Spirit
In the Heavens you are There
You're also here on the earth
Involved in our affairs

In Your Presence is fullness of joy
With You I'm complete
With You I can do all things
Any challenge I can meet

You hem me in behind before
I'm surrounded by Your love
Knowing You are with me
Walking with the Dove

Jehovah Shammah, always there!
You never leave us alone
Living our days here on earth
Longing for our heavenly home!

8.21.20

Names of God: El Shaddai - God Almighty (Genesis 17)

You are God Almighty
Your Name is El Shaddai
With You nothing's impossible
Miracles You supply!

Changed Abram to Abraham
Promised him an heir
Gave to him Isaac
Sarah's barren womb did bear

Age to Age You're still the same
Amy Grant sang
The song in the eighties
On our cassette players rang

In my time of trouble
El Shaddai, I look to you
with Your Mighty Power
I will have a breakthrough

El Shaddai El Shaddai
We lift Your Name of High!
Your Glory fills the earth!
Your Glory fills the sky!

8.16.20

Names of God: Adonai - Lord (Psalm 110)

You are Adonai
You are my Lord
I align my life to You
Living in accord

I gladly bow my knee
I gladly lift my hands
My soul delights
In Your Holy commands

Your commands are for my good
You do all things in love
Always seek the best
For those who are born of

the Spirit, we are citizens
Of the Kingdom of God
Living life eternal
While living abroad

Adonai how we love You!
May Your will be done
May our lives bring glory
Our lives have just begun!

8.16.20

Names of God: El Roi - The God Who Sees (Genesis 16)

Your Name is El Roi
You are the God Who Sees
You see with perfect clarity
Never miss the forest for the trees

You see into my heart
You see into my soul
You see my potential
Your Vision sees me whole

You look into my past
You give me a new start
You look into my future
Hope is off the charts!

You see with Kingdom eyes
Call things into being
Bring beauty from the ashes
In You life's so freeing!

El Roi help me see
Others as You do
Created in Your Image
Having utmost value!

8.17.20

The Names of God: El Elyon - God Most High (Isaiah 14)

Your Name is El Elyon
You are God Most High
Higher than all others
Cannot quantify

Your Might and Your Power
Your Glory fills the earth
If we could only see
Your magnificent worth!

High and Lifted Up
Isaiah caught a glimpse
Of You in Your Temple
Never the same since!

All of our problems
So small compared to You
Take down our Goliaths
Any slingshot will do

Seated on Your Throne
You are in Control
I'll be still and know
And praise You, O My Soul!

8.17.20

Names of God: El Olam - Everlasting God (Genesis 21)

You are the Everlasting God
Your Name is El Olam
Alpha and Omega
May Your Kingdom come

You created time
Know beginning from the end
You put eternity in our hearts
To yearn and apprehend

Our heart is restless till it finds
True rest comes from Thee
Knowing we were created
For Eternity

Our life is but a mist
Here today then gone
While body will decay
Our soul lives on and on

El Olam help me to know
And count my numbered days
Make my life count for Your glory
Following Your ways!

8.19.20

Names of God: Abba Father (Galatians 4:6)

Your Name is Abba Father
My heart cries out to You!
I am Your loving child
You're the One I look to

For security and peace
I'm in Your Loving Hands
In this crazy world
Where chaos rules the land

In You I find identity
Defined by Who You are
You call me Your beloved
You say I'm up to par

You sing over us, Your children
With Joy and Delight
Knowing You are with us
Helps us through the night

In You, Abba, we are free!
Free to live with glee!
Free to live abandoned lives
To live abundantly!

8.19.20

The I Am's of Jesus

This chapter of poems is focused on the seven "I AM" statements of Jesus found in the Gospel of John. They are an invitation to experience the different aspects of our Lord and Savior, Jesus Christ.

I AM the Bread of Life (John 6)

I AM the Bread of Life
That's come down from Heaven
Partake of Me
In Me there is no leaven

In the wilderness
Manna rained from the sky
When you believe in Me
You'll live and never die

Man shall not live
By eating bread alone
I overcame temptation
Not making bread from stone

There's plenty to eat!
You can eat this Bread for free!
Taste and see that I am good
Live Eternally!

I Am the Bread of Life
Come have a Slice!
When you dine with Me
You'll know Abundant Life!

7.21.20

I AM the Light of the Word (John 8)

I AM the Light of the World
I AM the Light of Life
My Light dispels the darkness
My Light quells the strife

In Me you can see!
My Light opens your eyes
Gives Revelation
Uncovers evil lies

How this world needs Light!
Racism and fear
Hatred and indifference
In the atmosphere

You are now the Light
Because I shine thru you
Let your good deeds
Show My Father's hue

I AM the Light of the World
When I am lifted high
Will draw the world to My Love
This love will not run dry!

7.21.20

I AM The Gate (John 10)

I AM the Gate for the sheep
Enter Thru My Grace
Into My Love and Goodness
Into a Spacious Place!

Into the Green Pastures
By the waters still
Graze to your heart's content
Resting in My will

The Open Gate is narrow
Come thru one at a time
Calling on My Name
Salvation you will find

Come into My care
In Me You shall not want
I'll tend to Your needs
In Me you won't be gaunt

All are invited to enter in!
My Arms are open wide
Enter thru The Gate
Your soul be satisfied!

7.22.20

I AM The Good Shepherd (John 10)

I AM The Good Shepherd
I care for My Sheep
I laid down My life
Salvation is not cheap

The hireling does not care
Is out for his own
Will always let you down
Will leave you all alone

My Sheep know My Voice
They won't be led astray
I know them each by name
I hear them when they pray

I can be Trusted
This truly is the Key
To our love relationship
Find your rest in Me

I AM The Good Shepherd
Come into my fold!
Here you'll find freedom
With blessings untold!

7.22.20

I AM The Resurrection and The Life (John 11)

The Resurrection and The Life
I AM the Great I AM
Lazarus in the grave
Obeyed my command

"Lazarus, come forth!"
He opened up His eyes
When you believe in Me
You'll live and will not die

The power of death
Has surely lost its sting
My Zoe Life will last
After Winter is Spring!

Resurrection Power
Lives within you Now
Victory is Yours
The enemy will bow

The Resurrection and The Life
I AM The Great I AM
Nothing is impossible
With Me in you, you can!

7.23.20

I AM the True Vine (John 15)

I AM the True Vine
Branches, cling to Me!
When you're disconnected
You live barrenly

Abide in Me and I in you
Connected at the heart
Bearing Fruit that will remain
Growth that's off the charts

I AM the Source of all that's good
Every good and perfect gift
When you are downcast
Your spirit I will lift

You are My servants
I also call you friends
Join My inner circle
To the nations I will send

Fulfill My Great Commission
Ride My Holy Wave
To gather in the Harvest
Souls to be saved!

7.26.20

I AM The Way, The Truth, and The Life (John 14)

I AM The Way
Come follow Me
I'll guide your steps
Joyfully

I AM The Truth
That you can know
More than a concept
In Me you'll grow

I AM The Life
That satisfies
Taste and see
I AM Your Prize

No other Way
But by Me
To the Father
Exclusively

Way Truth and Life
All these I AM
Believe in Me
And trust My Plan!

7.26.20

Who I Am In Christ

The Bible tells us that "if anyone is in Christ, the new creation has come: The old has gone, the new is here!" (2 Corinthians 5:17). We have a new identity in Christ! These poems focus on the many different wonderful identities we have as new creations in Christ!

I AM Your Beloved (Matthew 3:17)

I'm Your Beloved
On me Your Favor rests
You call me Your own
You call me Blessed

David understood
This Hesed love of God
Caused Him to sing
To dance and applaud

In a spacious place
Where we can run and play
In the fields of grace
We live free day by day

Loved unconditionally
Delighted in by You
Approval of the Father
I find my Value

I'm Your Beloved
Secure in Your Embrace
Loving heart to heart
Living Face to Face!

8.2.20

I Am a Child of God (1 John 3:1)

I am a Child of God
Abba, I am Yours
Fully loved by You
In You my spirit soars

Fearfully and wonderfully created
Your Image I do bear
Made in Your likeness
Made with Loving Care

As Your Child I trust
Your Promises are true
Knowing You are faithful
Testimonies accrue!

Let My Children come to Me
Let nothing hinder them
They have full access
To Heaven's ATM!

No place I'd rather be
Than in Your Loving Arms
My soul at peace and rest
Safe from all alarm!

8.26.20

I Am a Citizen of Heaven (Philippians 3:20)

Citizen of Heaven
This world is not my home
I'm just a passin thru
In this earthly zone

My passport reads the Kingdom
Got a visa for the earth
Joining in His Mission
For souls and their rebirth

The privileges are many
Being Citizens above
Relationship over rules
The currency is Love

Serving one another
The Kingdom is a place
Of treating others kindly
Of living Truth and Grace

All can be a Citizen
Jesus died for all!
Just call upon His Name
He'll surely hear your call!

8.27.20

I Am an Heir with Christ (Romans 8:17)

I am an Heir with Christ
Truly rich I am!
Blessed with every blessing
In Jesus' Name I can

Do all things thru His strength
His power that lives in me
I am content in everything
The power to simply be

No need to compare
Satisfied with my plight
In You I shall not want
I can travel light

Blessed with peace and joy and love
Endlessly supplied
Heart of gratitude
My soul is satisfied

My future is secure
My inheritance awaits
My inheritance is now
In Faith I activate!

8.28.20

I Am Blessed! (Psalm 1)

I am Blessed, I truly am!
Blessed by God above
#blessed is my domain
Living in His Love

Blessed to know my Creator
His Name is El Shaddai
When I call His Name
He sends power from on high!

Blessed to have a purpose
To do His Works on earth
It's my Who not my Do
That determines my worth

Blessed to love others
Love neighbor as myself
Living the Golden Rule
Keeps me in good health!

Blessed to be a Blessing!
To give better than to get
Live a life for others
And your own life will be set!

8.29.20

I Am His Ambassador (2 Corinthians 5:20)

I am His Ambassador
Chosen to represent
Appointed by the Father
To do His bidding sent

To this very place
Where I'm living now
Not a far off land
It's here I pull the plow

Work the land before me
Sowing Kingdom seeds
Actions more than words
Doing Kingdom deeds

This world needs to see Jesus
Who He truly is
He's so much better IRL (in real life)
When you're truly His

When He is lifted up
All people will be drawn
Singing forth His praise
We will wake the dawn!

8.31.20

We are the Body of Christ (Romans 12:5)

We are the Body of Christ
His hands and feet we are
While alone I can go fast
Together we go far!

Connected to the Head
Jesus is the Lord
May we be united
Living in one accord

Each part plays a role
Each part necessary
Helping one another
When we're feeling weary

As His Body we can change
The world for the better!
We are Salt and Light
We're His Living Letter!

Body of Christ arise!
It's time to take a stand
Proclaim the Name of Jesus
Revival in the Land!

9.2.20

We are the Family of God (Mark 3:35)

We are the Family of God
We are never alone
We stand with one another
We all live in One Home!

Brothers and sisters
We are Family!
We need to show the world
How to live in unity!

Our family allegiance
Greater than politics!
Greater than denominations
The Blood of Christ is thick!

In these crazy times
Our Family must shine
Overcoming hate
Showing Love Divine!

May the Lord's Face shine
On His Family below
Like Moses on the mountain
May our faces glow!

9.2.20

We are Salt and Light (Matthew 5:13-16)

We are Salt and Light
Placed in the earth
To bring out God flavors
To shine forth His Great Worth

A single grain of salt
Cannot effect much change
Many grains together
Can totally rearrange

The world as it is
Bring it rightside up
When we join together
Show the world wassup!

Out of the salt shaker
Placed wisely by the Lord
Sharing the Good News
Leading others toward

An encounter with God
The Resurrected King
Salt and Light, it's time
To do your thing!

9.14.20

I Am His Creation (Genesis 1:26)

I am His Creation
Created to create
Made in God's Image
I now participate

I'm working with the Master
His Kingdom work I do
Fills my life with meaning
Won't you join Him too?

He says I am His Masterpiece
Hanging in the Louvre
On my life He's signed His Name
My worth don't need to prove

My value comes from God
The fact that I am His
Don't live by this world's standards
I know what time it is!

We all reflect His beauty
Says to us "very good"
Feel His Smile upon us
Loved and understood!

9.4.20. Yosemite Lodge

We are His Peacemakers (Matthew 5:9)

We are His Peacemakers
Called to bring His Peace
In the midst of trials
May His peace increase!

Called to understanding
Called to listen first
Called to love our neighbor
Before the trouble bursts!

Our country is divided
Nations are at war
The future seems uncertain
Who knows what's in store?

Covid's killing many
The cure is yet in sight
Who can bring us comfort
From this scary plight?

We know the One who knows
The answer to these ails
He is the Prince of Peace
He surely will prevail!

9.12.20

We are a Royal Priesthood (1 Peter 2:9)

We are His Royal Priesthood
His calling we must keep
Stand with the oppressed
Weep with those who weep

The priest in the parable
Didn't even care
When his neighbor was bleeding
Acted like he wasn't there

Samaritan in the story
Loved his neighbor well
Bound up his wounds
Paid for his motel

Our Black brothers and sisters
Are suffering right now
We will listen and care
Indifference not allow

May Your Kingdom come
Lord here on this earth
Till each and every person
Esteemed for their great worth

9.24.20

We are a Holy Nation (1 Peter 2:9)

We are a Holy Nation
Citizens of Heaven
A people set apart
Rid of the world's leaven

In these times of division
United we must stand
Allegiance to the Kingdom
In Christ we must band

Together as His people
Bonded by His Blood
When we are divided
His Name's dragged thru the mud

We're not of this world
We belong to the King
Called to share the Good News
To every person bring

A Light unto the World
May our Good Deeds shine
Known for love and kindness
We are a Kingdom sign!

9.18.20

We are Living Letters (2 Corinthians 3:3)

We are Living Letters
Written with Christ's ink
Our hearts are His tablets
Our lives are the link

For others to know Jesus
Thru us He makes appeal
Demonstrating His Kingdom
Loving and keepin it real

Lord here is my pen!
Please, freely write!
I give You full control
You have my green light

Not my will but Thine
My own Gethsemane
Trusting in Your way
You know better than me!

May this Living Letter
Be a testimony
Of Your Great Faithfulness
Of Your Great Love story!

9.16.20

We Are His Holy Temple (Ephesians 2:21)

We are His Holy Temple
The Spirit dwells in me
Not a physical building
We're a people who are set free

In the days of Moses
The Tabernacle the place
In the Holy of Holies
Was where you sought God's Face

When Jesus came to earth
The Living Tabernacle
The Word made flesh who dwelt with us
Breaking people's shackles

After Pentecost
The Spirit was poured out
To live inside each one of us
His Kingdom bring about

From this Holy Temple
The world is reached through us
Declaring forth His praises
Make His Name glorious!

9.17.20

I Am God's Friend (John 15:15)

God has called me friend
Can it really be?
The God of the Universe
Friends with little ole me?

I'll take it by faith
Say yes to the call
And grow into friendship
With the Lord of all

Jesus calls me friend
Shares with me His heart
Wants to hang with me!
His secrets to impart

Not a "friend" on Facebook
This friendship's IRL
Two way messaging
Speed dial on my cell

What a friend I have in Jesus
No more need to fret!
He's got me covered!
With Him my life is set!

9.18.20. Malibu Prayer Retreat

We are God's Army (2 Timothy 2:4)

We wrestle not
With flesh and blood
When the enemy comes
In like a flood

We raise a standard
The Cross of Christ
His Victory
His Sacrifice

In Jesus Name
We rebuke our foe
We'll win the battle
For we know

The enemy
Has been defeated!
In heavenly places
We are seated

Hear God's Army!
Time to arise!
Hallelujah!
Our battle cry!

9.20.20

His Sheep Am I (John 10:27)

I am His lamb
His sheep am I
I'm in His care
On Him rely

The Lord my Shepherd
I shall not want
Before I knew him
Was frail and gaunt

Now I am content
Fed by His Word
in Green pastures
Future's assured

Though I wander
Easily stray
He leaves the ninety nine
Makes sure I'm okay

I love to be His sheep!
My Shepherd is the best!
In this crazy world
Am peaceful and at rest!

10.12.20

I Am a Jar of Clay (2 Corinthians 4:7)

I am a jar of clay
On the Potter's wheel
Being shaped by Him
It's so hard to be still!

He is the Master Potter
He knows the best design
I think that I know better
I complain and I whine

I question His plan
I question His time
It's all part of shaping
This sinful heart of mine

I release control
Help me Lord to trust
Help me to surrender
Remember I'm but dust

Lord there is freedom!
On Your Potter's Wheel
Shape this jar of clay
Your Glory reveal!

10.8.20

We are Christ's Aroma (2 Corinthians 2:15)

We are Christ's aroma
We carry Heaven's scent
The fragrance of Jesus
His Kingdom represent

In this world that's dying
Where hope is wearing thin
We're called to change the atmosphere
His power's breaking in!

Breathing in His goodness
Breathing out His grace
The beauty of the Lord
Filling up this space

Unfailing love of God
Exuding from our pores
May our testimony
Be an open door

For others to behold
The Glory of the King
The aroma of worship
Changing everything!

10.8.20

I Am His Servant (Matthew 23:11)

I am His loving servant
Following His steps
Washing the feet of others
Showing ALL respect

When I care for others
I do it unto Him
I lay down my ego
Over selfishness must win!

In the act of serving
Am so close to my Lord
I can feel His heartbeat
Living in one accord

Holy Spirit fill me
Open up my eyes
So many are in need
Help me realize

In this world where self
Is always number one
I'm trying to change the narrative
May His will be done!

10.20.20

I am His Disciple (Luke 9:23)

I am Christ's disciple
Jesus is My Lord
What He says I'll do
Following His Word

Jesus is my Teacher
I'll learn life from Him
To live life abundantly
Fill it to the brim!

Following His footsteps
WWJD?!
Listening for His voice
So attentively

Living in His Presence
Enjoying fellowship
Intimacy and friendship
Is discipleship!

The call to make disciples
Is my life's sole mission
To bear fruit for His Glory
Is my life's ambition!

10.19.20

We are ONE! (John 17)

Father make them One
Was Jesus' prayer
That the world would know You sent Me
The world would know you care

Lord make us One!
Break down our divisions
We are United
The Cross our provision

Unity not uniformity
We are diverse
Loving one another
Reversing the curse!

Higher allegiance
To Jesus our Lord
Not to this world
The Kingdom moving forward!

By this all will know
We're Your disciples
We love one another
May Your love go viral!

10.18.25

I Am A Worshipper (John 4:24)

I Am a Worshipper
In Spirit and in truth
Worshipping Him
From the days of my youth

Only God is worthy
Of all my praise
He is unchanging
He is Good Always

God fights our battles
He is always for us
Join with the angels
Join Heaven's chorus

All tribes and tongues
Join round the Throne
Singing praise to Jesus
Our Chief Cornerstone

Hallelujah!
Give glory to One!
Worshippers rejoice!
The Victory is Won!

10.21.20

Made in the USA
Columbia, SC
16 December 2020

28251508R00093